Counting
with animal friends

by Dorothy McCluskey

First edition 2023

ISBN: 979-8-35091-778-9

The illustrations for this book were created using gouache and colored pencil.

Printed in the USA on FSC and SFI Certified paper

To Liam, Maya and Luke....
May you always follow your dreams.

Love, Nonnie

1

One happy hippo
Loving her spread
Grunting and snoring
Asleep in her bed

2

Two furry bears
Ready to fish
Sitting on logs
Just making a wish

Three piggyback pigs
Standing so tall
Keeping their balance
Before they all fall

4

Four dainty raccoons
By the deep blue sea
Chattin' and slurpin'
All sipping their tea

5

Five funny owls
In the night sky
One getting sleepy
One saying "Hi"

6

Six crowin' roosters
Wakin' up at dawn
Cock-a-doodle doosters
No time to yawn

7

Seven honey bees
Their buckets a holdin'
Laden with sweetness
The nectar so golden

8

Eight fancy flamingos
Necks crooked n' pink
Legs put on backwards
What do you think?

9

Nine downy ducks
Birds of a feather
Out on a pond
In all kinds of weather

10

Ten perky penguins
Eating a treat
Ice cream's their favorite
Drippin' on their feet

About the Artist

The studio of Dorothy McCluskey is a place of imagination and whimsy, where the artist creates vibrant Santa Clauses, builds fairy houses, and paints illustrations that come to life in young minds. With the publication of Counting with Animal Friends, Dorothy welcomes you to join in her world of animal fun!

With "special thanks" to Jeanne and Bruce for sharing their time and magical talents.